Dedicated to the bees.

Starfish Bay® Children's Books
An imprint of Starfish Bay Publishing
www.starfishbaypublishing.com

DEE THE BEE

© Dolores Keaveney, 2020
ISBN 978-1-76036-096-2
First Published 2020
Printed in China

Sincere thanks to Elyse Williams from Starfish Bay Children's Books for her creative efforts in preparing this edition for publication.

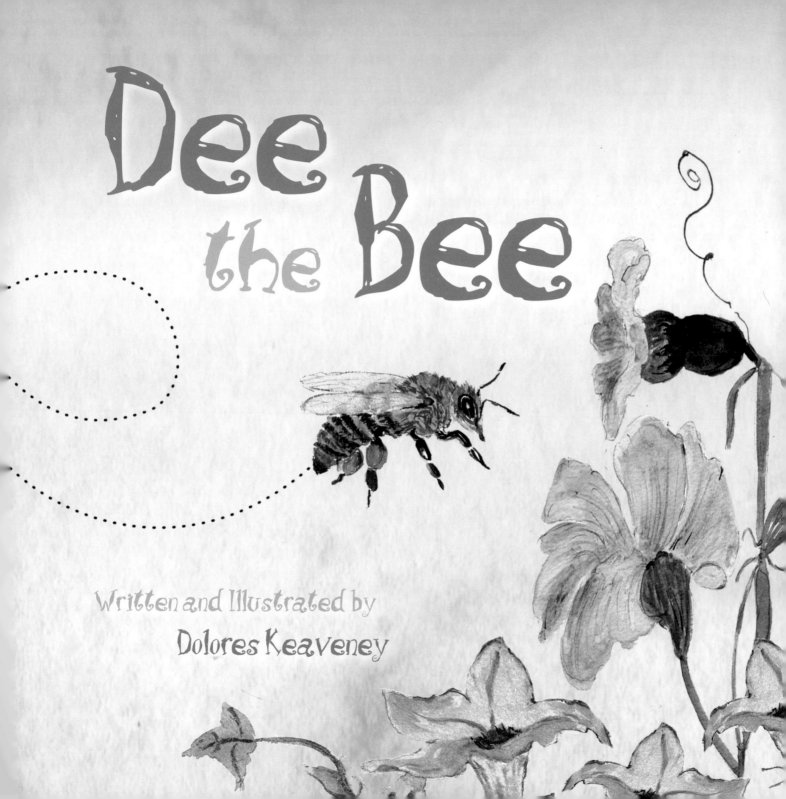

# Dee the Bee

Written and Illustrated by

Dolores Keaveney

If I were a bee,
        I'd pollinate and play
in the fruits, the herbs
        and veggies
                we eat every day.

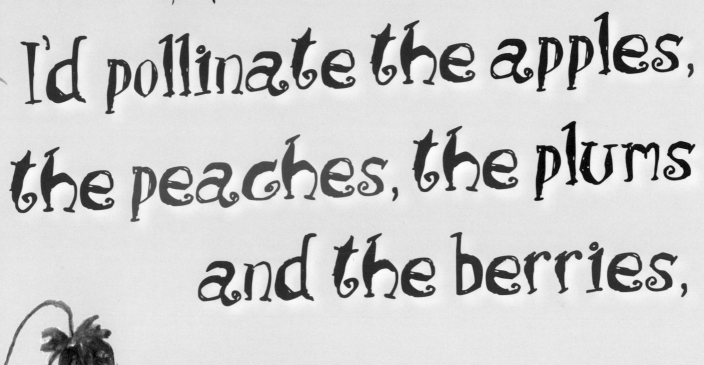

I'd pollinate the apples, the peaches, the plums and the berries,

the limes, the lemons
and the grapes,
the pears, the rhubarb
and the cherries.

I'd pollinate the turnips,

the pumpkins and the peppers,

the chestnuts,
    leeks and onions,
the radishes
    and cucumbers.

I'd pollinate the Brussels sprouts,

the
cabbage
and the celery,

the nuts,

the spices,

and

the beans,

the carrots
and the
broccoli.

If I were out
collecting food,
I'd never make a sound.
I'd pick up pollen on my legs
and spread
it all around.

When the pollen drops inside the flower,

it mingles

with the

seed.

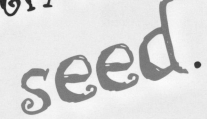

This is how
you get
the fruit.

It's
magical
indeed.

So, now you see
it's down to me
to pollinate all these.
You'll not have any
fruit to eat
if you haven't got the bees.

Yes, it's me.
My name is Dee.

I am a little
honey bee.

# Pollination, pollination, pollination,
## a very big word for consideration.

1. As the bee visits a flower to collect food, pollen from stamens stick to its body.

Pollen

2. The bee then flies to another flower of the same type.

Just look down below, read easily and slow,
and you'll get the full explanation.

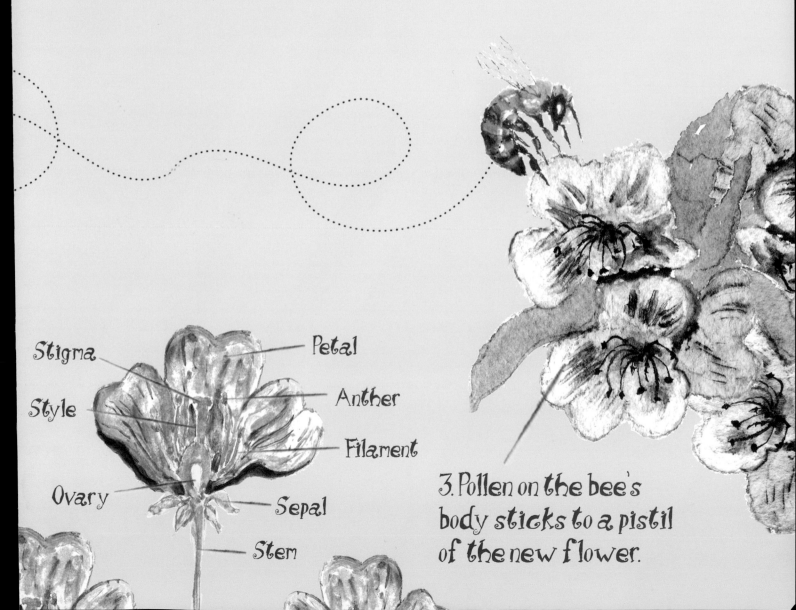

Stigma

Style

Ovary

Petal

Anther

Filament

Sepal

Stem

3. Pollen on the bee's
body sticks to a pistil
of the new flower.

# Plant these flowers in your

Delphinium

Red Clover

Purple Cone Flower

Lavender

Vetch

Foxglove

# garden to welcome in the bees.

**Poppies**

**Dandelion**

**Buddleia**

**Bluebell**

**Sunflower**

**Black-eyed Susie**